FATHER INDIA

"A groundbreaking work....an indispensable book. "
—Bharati Mukherjee, *San Francisco Chronicle*

"I admire Father India immensely. I don't quite know how Jeffery Paine has done it except by subtle and provocative genius....a splendid achievement."
—Denis Donoghue, Henry James Professor of English and American Letters, New York University

"Jeffery Paine's *Father India* is a work of extraordinary scope and quality.....Its pages breathe with the intelligence of an exceedingly good writer and a masterly critic."
—John Lukacs, author of 35 books, including *A Thread of Years* and *Confessions of an Original Sinner*

"A bold thesis, stylishly argued....a book both challenging and enjoyable."
—*The Washington Times*

RE-ENCHANTMENT: TIBETAN BUDDHISM COMES TO THE WEST

"Jeffery Paine is an unusual voice in American letters—one steeped in the wisdom of the East and yet infused with a knowing and witty sensibility that is profound Western. *Re-enchantment* is a delight, a work of education and demystification that instructs and entertains on every page."
—Shashi Tharoor, author of *The Great Indian Novel* and Under-Secretary General of the United Nations

"Marvelous! This is just the book on Buddhism I hoped someone would write but was afraid they never would. Paine captures the powerful, sometimes zany but electric atmosphere generated by the arrival of Buddhism on these shores....this is also a great read."
—Harvey Cox, author of *The Secular City* and Hollis Professor of Divinity, Harvard University

"Lucid and slyly humorous, Paine's effortless prose is that of a writer who knows his material extremely well and can make thru reader share his respect and fondness for the practitioners of one of the fastest growing religions in the United States."
—Sudhir Kakakr, author of *Shamans, Mystics, and Doctors*

"Jeffery Paine is a sharp-eyed and soul-active writer. *Re-enchantment* brings us a perspective we badly need in our unsettled hour."
—Sven Birkerts, author of *My Sky Blue Trades*

ADVENTURES WITH THE BUDDHA: A PERSONAL BUDDHISM READER
"Paine's real genius is constructing a coherent, potent anthology that informs, delights, and fires the imagination, a work that both recovers a lost world and illustrates its continued relevance today."
—*Publishers Weekly* (starred review)

"*Adventures with the Buddha* eloquently distills the essence of Buddhism through nine of the greatest minds spanning three generations. Jeffery Paine, once again, offers an enchanting and powerful learning tools for students of Buddhism."
—Tulku Thondup, author of *The Healing Power of Mind*

"Highly enjoyable....Recommended."
—*Library Journal*

"*Adventures with the Buddha* is filled with stories of Westerners who have experienced mysteries, marvels, exotic discomforts, fabled temples, and that's only the half of it. Then the internal adventures begin...as absorbing as stories from the romantic past, showing that the most exciting explorations take place within minds and hearts."
—Booknotes

ENLIGHTENMENT TOWN
"In *Enlightenment Town* Jeffery Paine takes us on a journey to meet [the town's] unforgettable inhabitants in Airstream trailers, disused mine shafts, and quiet retreats, across nineteen years. Fascinating, beautifully written, often funny, sometimes weird—you will love this modern Thoreau."
—Nigel Hamilton, award-winning biographer of JFK, Thomas Mann, Bill Clinton, FDR, and others

"As Jeffery Paine insinuates, even those of us who are "postreligious" nonetheless seek some "hallowed understanding" of the human condition. Paine writes such vivid stories about Crestone's eclectic spiritual characters that I have to confess, that I am charmed beyond belief."
—Kai Bird, Pulitzer Prize-winning biographer of Robert Oppenheimer and Jimmy Carter

"What if Thornton Wilder had read *The Tibetan Book of the Dead* before writing *Our Town*?... What if Billy Graham had befriended Allen Ginsberg and they had done ayahuasca together? This is the sort of wild nowhere/everywhere American landscape that Jeffery Paine describes with great flair, courage, and insight in Enlightenment Town."
—Dana Sawyer, author of *Houston Smith and The Transcendental Meditation Movement*

"Enlightenment Town is a generous, delightful book, full of divine misfits and quasi-saints who have dared—or been forced—to widen their (and our) horizons. You won't be able to resist Jeffery Paine's openness to this community, nor his sly proposal that spiritual life can be gentler and quite a bit wilder."
—Kate Wheeler, meditation teacher and prize-winning author of *Not Where I Started From* and *When Mountains Walked*

Eternity,
Speak
With This Living Man

Jeffery Paine

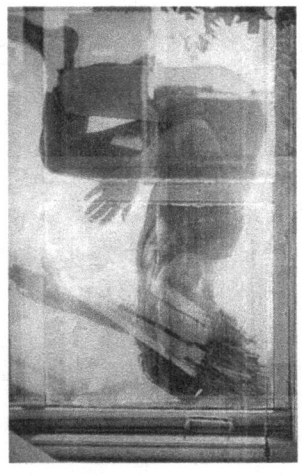

SPUYTEN DUYVIL
New York City

Acknowledgments

to tt
unique among publishers

to AKM, Jr.
Visionary

and to SMS
who uses poetry, among other things,
to transform existence into sacredness.

To Professor CC
Jnana yogi, Bhakti yogi, and Karma yogi—all

CONTENTS

The Victrola Hummed Merrily

If with too much wine,
serene, you imagine
        pure music: a long liquid note,
                then it was such a sound
                which the slow knife found
        and spilled endlessly from his throat.

Eternity, speak with this dead man.
Tell him now of the woman you never loved.

The Face At Fifty

Twelve Tales

I. A Surprise

The chance turn on the chance street corner - -
Unexpected silver in a shop windowglass.
Oh my god!

II. No Theory of Aesthetics

The broken nose slashes, slants off at raggedy angle,
With disdain mocks the principles of symmetry,
Mocks aesthetics, and my poor and former vanity.

And the sheer weight of the face,
Avalanche of flesh, an incipient second chin -
A soft cow's stomach.

The boast of the man at age 30:
"Always a little fatter, always balding,
But ever to remain handsome,

That, and that alone, is the Contract."
At 50, it's deemed legally non-binding.
Torn up — shredded egos flecking the wind.

III. NOW AND THEN

I need a haircut.
Well, Einstein needed a haircut
(Who's coming unglued, just 'cause the mess is going wild?)

Once, a mother wept to see these curls cut.
Once, the shampoo—sinuous and sensual—
Traced in every curl a voluptuous trajectory.

IV. REMEMBER AT ALL TIMES YOUR GREATNESS

What does the face look like
Of the man or woman
Who has read Shakespeare, Homer, and Yeats?

What does the face look like
Of the man or woman
Who has looked upon Piero, Yosemite, and the daily sun?

What does the face look like
Of the man or woman
Who has pronounced the word "God" 100,000 times?

V. Your Father's Moustache

My moustache is an anachronism from history:
Thomas Dewey and the sly American meanness,
The playboys and villains of fiction and fashion.

Mainly I see the moustache of my sweet lost father
Who shaved it off only once, while his son
Wondered at the living infinity scarcely acted upon.

Before his last illness, my father reached that stage
Where actions are only supportive, softly nodded, *Yes,*
Kindness and generosity his whole last act.

Thus the planes relax, contours soften
When we live right, until our face to other faces turns
Solely curious, amical, and handsome with care.

VI. Resurrection

But oh, the tired look of my face this evening:
Generations born and died, born and died,
Arching through endless time seem not so tired

As the eternal circles under the eyes, the eyes
Which are cavities, the cavities which are bruises;
Two inches above the mouth, behind whose lips

The tongue, an actor waiting in the wings,
Moist with expectation, slips to the wet mouth
Rehearsing: *Something yet will happen.*

VII. At the Congress of Facial Studies

1st Delegate (a writer-friend):
   "First, your face physically has volume, and by volume I mean
   Sound, volume.
   Secondly, by your eyes the volume attenuates. Two green lakes at
   peace.
   Then the mouth betrays itself, intelligent and cruel."

   2nd Delegate (a painter-friend):
      "A chipmunk with a moustache and black curly hair."

      3rd Delegate (my girlfriend):
   "The form is classical and Grecian, with but the slightest flaw to
   sweeten it. The olive skin is a Greek island, under blue skies. And
   the lips and the mouth . . . better not get me started."

VIII. Spooks Have Eyebrows?

   I lament how my eyebrows have grown bare,
   How not being there is also a way of being there,
   As if life were anything but ghosts having affairs.

IX. From P.-P. Rubens to A. Renoir

   The skin will be complemented by cotton pastel shirts:
   On your arm, by pastel women;
   Destination, promenading the spring-hued earth.

   Dermatologists and gourmands hypothize water
   Under the skin: "The good life is to be alive.
   The good life is good skin, to be fat and rosy."

X. Movie Metaphors

Oh my stars, in what films could this face be cast?
The Man Who Was Half Lucky In Love.
Shamed, Saddened, Shat Upon, But Ne'er Defeated.

"Sorry, Kid, we're not casting your type
Any more." "Frankly, my dear sir,
I don't give a damn."

XI. The Under-side of the 18th Century

Burp. Drool. Cough. Blink. Scratch.
Fart. Twitch. Belch. Pant. Spasm.
Our eccentricities, ourselves, are out of control.

XII. The Argonauts

In charitable light, in darkness or distance,
  At angle merciful—for a moment no lines
  Appear to mar the surface anywhere:

The skin, flushed adolescent pools,
The sails full, the wind,
As of yore, gusts on the shore.

Excess of fret, excess of pleasure,
Much shame overcome:
The history of the face at 50.

The Komische Casa Of Dr. Wittgenstein

Wittgenstein's Apartment

Wittgenstein's rooms begrudge the furniture in them,
Every chair bearing the impossible weight of
A history of associations, a constriction of existence,
And him the secret guest, living like a squatter.

The lares—the gods of the household—are dead, Sir:
What the uncommonly silly call "common sense"—
The comfortable and deceiving long way round to death—
May no longer be subscribed to, even should the philosopher want to.

The Universe of the Philosophers

This is the world of the philosophers
(But *you'll* lack the courage to enter):
The accidental and the incidental, the cozy hum,
Gossip, all that's foible, sssh's still and mum;

Only some abstract purity—pure as pain—
Chatters no lies. Or is that too a language game,
E. g. emotional and physical aches hardly the same
Yet both answer to pain, an identical name.

Chalk screeches on blackboards, pens drops from the hand
In Wittgenstein's classes, in rooms made of words:
There it is decided and never decided
Whether sound or silence, body or mind, is more derided.

THE BODY OF WORK

Wittgenstein's body was thin and trim,
Fasting or feasting on hard bread to the end
Of sloppy thinking; to sloppy living, let there be an end.
The philosopher warms no comfort sans proof or theorem.

Age or pain screech in his body,
A greedy fist of needles scooping up coins of excruciation
In a mesh of muscles (and not minding too much),
Which leaves him stoic even in decimation.

It's so easy to be above everything, and so hard.

READER'S LIEDER

Here, the Reader nodding late,
Droopy eyes dropping, notes his corpulent state,
Body overweight, wondering over his wine
How different is he from Wittgenstein?

In your sink are dirty dishes,
Days there maybe, but, yum, it was delicious;
Oh yours is not the komische casa sublime
Of Wittgenstein, St. Wittgenstein

Thermometer: 97°F

As easy as to sigh is to sit, collapse in a stuffy bus
While the wheels roll forward. Head against the hot glass,
      to believe that you sleep or that you're awake, it's choice.
          Example: myself, city image/
          Purgatorial image, the melted pane.
      La vida es sueño. No, no, not a dream,
For dreams too sway to rules. The stifling bus just rolls forward,
      like mercury in thermometers spurting up.

That good men move, or psychiatrists' words help, crumbles
Cinematic illusion, that is better called "a memory".
      That good women will recall, or there are
          bumblebees in the brain, these—bzzz—
          are unofficial fancies: Nothing's
      accepted, nothing's rejected, when sweat
Of languor works the acid on, when rusty thermometers
      supersede cold lies cold men despaired were "real".

Herr Dr. Freud invented the superego, Saint Alpha-
Bet wrote a sermon on moral obligation. This happened
      long ago in Wien, a cold city. Here, *one*
          sins or not, as they like. Climb six
          flights of stairs, thumb through the Bible:
      no sermons get said in the tropics. Wrongdo-
Er and angelic messenger confuse who's who, as both here
      lie prostrate, sipping lemonade from the fridge.

Ascend now the lenient senses, Then lay summer seen
And heard. Touch it. Taste! Badboy's baptism at the fire
      hydrant: Motored fans purr or snore: Small
          'squeeter-breezes playful on a brown skin:

Ice cream on white plates, the fictive
soul made visible.   Laugh, or cry. True Salvation
Would barge in on a colder day; good men, though they will
rejoice, neither stop nor start to invent it.

Renaissance Air

At fifteen Tom learnt the physicke for bodies,
At twenty to master the legal tedium that steadies
A realm; at twenty-three his studies seemed complete. Dr.
Campion knew now, in a nut, everything.
                              That fair ladies,
Loose laughter, fast friends, and good poetry
Were pleasant.   Their contraries—lawyers hawking phlegm,
Dull disputes of may-be versus might-be, and haglike women
With coughs—less so.
                              To-who! To-woo!
                              From owlish throats
                              A wooing note.

          To ravish human sense, the human senses drowned;
          Sister, who so kills? The sweet delighting viol,
                              With its murderous melodious rounds.
          To manufacture light conceits for lovers
          Brother, let us—while sonnets and sonatas
                              Spread over us their secret cover.

His poetry he called the superfluous blossoms
Of a deeper study. Publish them who will,
Loot them if you like, lute them as you like;
Sing them well, then he might claim them;
If harshly, then away he'd give them.
Such was his prescription.
                              His medicine—a song,
That physicke that clears the vapors in human breasts,
Opening the pipe, it cools the heart, warms the wit,
Pronunciation refines, the stammerer it corrects;
And supplies that needed blissful note,
As a prayer in the churchyard of the owls.

To who! To-woo!
A wooing note.

Hummed at work and by play lulled
Laborers with hammers, barbers with scissors;
Tinkers sang catches, milkmaids ballads,
At dinner, at supper;
The viol hung in shops, the lute was the library;
Carters whistled; the beggar knew his straine
At marriages and dyings, At night and by dawn.

To who! To-woo!
A wooing note.

THE CATERPILLAR IMPERATIVE

Things are as they are and things change
Your mother's not dead—she's Monday

Stare till firm the image in the mirror
You turn, it goes blank like sorrow

What matters if you misunderstand
The tried and the true are not your friends

Any book you thumb through may explain it
All right: it is someone else who reads it

Youth to age, well to ill, foul to fair, no to yes:
This, said the worm, is Wonderland.

THE CIVICS TEACHER

At her desk she slouched, yet poised,
Girlishly, though somehow no girl.

A half hour I talked and talked,
Of what? Not even I heard.

The blackboard was time-haunted,
All words in starry chalk doubled.

Then rang the bell. Alone. The teacher failed!
My desk was papered in a mess of essays, clichés

And the paper memory of flesh, under a classroom bulb.
Upon my weight fell the weight of light.

Bethlem Royal Hospital

For D. A.

the author of Hell

Once maybe dreaming maybe drunk, I saw myself.. knot
...naught...Not!
big-bosomed, covered with testicles
Croaking messiah-speak that none could understand.

Washing in water never so wet as foul
Dribbling drooling over bowls of inedibles
Changing universes rather than underwear

But why flaunt this jewelry of pain
Comedies become tragedies, tragedies turn into comedy
like a snake coiling round, an argument forever tedious

Come, regard yourself in the mirror no one there
Trapped between walls and doors and no metaphors
Am I inside out? when *to be* and *ago* mix any which way

Will I find the way gaily to live
Amid chains and filth—Bedlam it's called—
Even as mad filthy as I

MEDIEVAL TAPESTRIES

Out of moth's acid-mouthed books she stirred,
Who shivered white winter under one pricking fur,
Whose bareness made blight her nakedness beneath,
Where her fingers feigned a false vow, the ague and the grief.
Penitent fingers fled that stench-luring womb,
And, sitting by fires, she lent them to loom.

She knit the fair unicorn. Desire
Declined in her flanks. Horn at fantasy's tip
Pits chips in the white ice of winter as it twists
Into her twitching fevers; Break cracks
Where groans the high-horned unicorn, and her unfrozen
Moans, like cats' meowings, dampen in the throat:
Perspiration boiling a wash of hairshead desire
And woolly Horse into heat. High-hot, steam-sweated:
Lusty bubbles lift up, liquor off the body,
Pearly sweaty, damp—and a cry unheard for water, breath:
Weave, weave, oh tapestry, weave.

In a dream tapestry dreamt by sinners,
Cumbrous boiling bodies on a sodden mattress,
Together, alone, where no wind will wind,
Insinuates a mazy, murky phantasmagoria:
An ivory Eye pierces the humid imperfection—
Mystic, manic—even as the burning cities catch fire,
Even unto the expiration of desire.

My love and I drowsed in duskingtide:
Coo of the bones, fleshing out flesh, the tongue tasting shadow places.
My Love accompanied my love through dusk and dark,
Her long spun-out hair tapestried my shoulders.
Lie, lie down once more, light the lamp, in the darkening city.

Old, we make a tapestry of what once was—
Monohorned beasts and memento mori and perfection of desire—
Found, and fading, in olden tomes and obsolete forms.

Snowflake Unalike

As a single silver snowflake
Melted into the rusty garden rake
I grasped how intricately might move
                    an imp, a me
Moved by impotent lust for you.

Neither Emily Dickinson Nor La Belle Otero

What   (?)
   You!

         are is

she ate
                  her words hurriedly

   You are Nothing

                              Less

                        than a line of poetry
                        than a lion of poetry
Which made him
         fidget

                        What then are my feet?

Toupees I guess
            she guessed

                        wildly

Her knowledge   (of)

                  anatomy was frightening

and concerning metre even worse

AUGUST 23, 1927 (A CENTURY AGO)

It's chic to be a sheik,
not too expensive either.   Admission?
                              Perdition
   for the ladies, five cents for gents.
Ah Rudolpho Alfonzo Raffaelo Giovanni Guglielmi—
Wop Salad!   Scusi, scusi.   a wop, a jew, a wop
                                      pop corn and soda pop
                                      Melt in the melting pot

To us he's all but forgot
Supposedly he cut a sort of cross
(jesus, wouldn't he be cross)
between Clara Bow and Sacco
        (weren't the Twenties a bunny?)
                pretty bay-be, pretty bay-be
Oops! A dirty depression apple big as a melon
        (Andrew) The Decline of the West (Mae)
                Boop boo pee doop
Rudolph o Rudolph o-o-o Rudy
        jada jada jada

Dead notes, a broken piano, the nickelodeon shut.

Coos Mrs Calvin Coolidge, coy,
To Mr Calvin Coolidge, cool:
"Wasn't that Valentino cad
Simply too disgraceful, Cal?"

                    It went whispered:
                        he seemed sensual
                        to ladies menstrual.

"He was swell at the Majestic".
"Everyone sighed and Toots was crying"
"It's no good trying your hand at denying"
"When the majestic sheik makes them shriek"
Here's a brand new code for a brand new industry:
Blood or/and tits. The second American Revolution
settles in; declares all men born
are born free and sexual. The Spirit of '76
lies down, it rolls over
to the spirit of 69 (Club).
It's the old George III-D.H. Lawrence controversy—
who wrote whom? Still no income tax,
no war in Asia yet. But to be *both_*
married and have under hot lights to make movies!
"I don't like it," whined Valentino.

In the newsreels Hoover
        began to resemble Christ (but fatter) ;
Newspaper headlines sang of the two
        Italian anarchists: "Guilty Guilty Death Penalty!"
While in "Modern Times" the Little Fellow suffered it
        all once again—though now nobody spoke at all.

In the outer alphabet, among the V-signs,
Besides Bartolomeo Vanzetti's, inscribe this name,
Insert a still fading photograph.
Accept: at last heart become acceptable,
This red valentine for Rudolph Valentino,
For he too loved and tried and failed and died,
As the crime from memory fades.

MY SWEET PAPA'S IDEA FOR POETRY

Dear
Dad,
Who
Never
Thought
To
Write
One,
Had
a
Daft
Plan
for
a
Poem:
Each
Line
Would
Have
but
One
Sound,
no
More
no
Less.

Here
It
Is[1],
Dad.

---

1 With
No
Rhyme
and
No
Feet
It
Went
No
Place.
Too
bad;—
But
What
can
one
Say?

MARILYN MONROE AND THE BACHELOR

But hey you! Yes, you
With not even a little bitch of a shrew-wife—
Without sex and scant remembrance of sex,
No sex to unhex the dull day's decline.
Dragging home from work
You're cruddy, you're unbelievable,
An airy-fairy monk of air or fantasy,
Sustaining your juices in a straight line,
Instead of the shutdown-startup modality
Of those who succeed by day
And copulate or raise children by night.
You deny the problematicalness of life
By forgetting to think about it.

Where did she of all womankind learn sexuality?
The ancients called it? *pseudo-dioneysian?*
The compensatory plunge into the solo,
The semi-erotic and the excess, the almost impersonal
Orgy of unintegrated groans, onomatopoeic moans,
So many lost layers to find your way back through,
With inaudible cries like little fishes biting at the surface,
A surface without will, faint as on old man's orgasm.
Little wonder from day to day the day-to-day
Meanders, turns, and returns, rigid and chore-bound,
When only our reverie is fertilized.

You have yet to learn to,
To spread yourself like oil over troubled water.
You are a bachelor, phone book in hand,
Confused by the multiplicity of many names.
Images on a screen, near, adoring, shine not near—
Remote as a spinster-authoress living alone
Whose plots are trivial but she makes them sound grand:
Jee-sus! Ordinarily only paramours render one another
The fret and the release she/you accomplish under cover.

You make love in the afternoon, and gray is the weather.

THE LUXURIOUSNESS OF UXORIOUSNESS

He said his wife's silky, pillowy breasts
    were his velvety cushions made in Brabant
        his camping out in the hills of Nature
            his adult infant's bottle, dreamy drunkenness

He boasted that his logic followed her lacey slip
    as a dog its young master
        as the tides the moon's blonde urging
            as a teen follows TikTok

He claimed her Mona-Lisan-plus smile vanquished
    traffic lines of road-rage commuters
        knives sharpened for suicide
                Mason-Dixon lines wherever civil wars never end

He chimed, "A married man always has something to think about."
But to think was one thing
    he was afraid to ,
        afraid to do,
            he was afraid to.

WHILE THE EPIDEMIC RAGED

At the very last, the invitation arrived.
My tiny intentions—the home improvements, career promotion,
The New Year's resolution to be a better person—now desert me,
Fast as rats. It's too easy to learn to mourn
Extinction of what you never learned to love.

    Where is the epidemic? It is everywhere.
    The newspaper print is brighter reporting it.
    Every conversation lends it habitation. Every friend of a friend
    Knows personally a victim. Now the day seems gray for a reason.
    And so we live, and so we live, half fearing for our reason.

I've had a good life, a rich life—so I've said.
The quaint hotel I managed. Bodies like supine statuary in my bed.
Everyone saves my funny letters. I'm not opposed to dying—
So I said. But worry cautions me back, it seems,
Back to where I have not yet begun to live.

Should I clasp tenderly the hand of one sicker
His brow dab with cooling water; nights, read Buddhist scripture.
But this "sainthood" retreats into my private solitude,
Not meant for lights, camera, action. Besides, what if God
Shrewd and easily angered, should disdain my cut-rate bargain?

So now I must begin my new profession
In status, below the garbageman's. And I'm not an Oriental
Where death's considered a big adventure. Exhausted, afraid,
Yet for the first time mixed with unexpected gratitude,
Like an Amish farmer tasting the sweetness of ripe vegetables.

"CITY PIGEONS, YUCK—"

Salvation by works and feathers?
this gray wavering
over gray cement?

Their speech, their song
Warble warble nauseous warble - -
acoustically annoying.

Our spring is their winter.
Our winter is their winter,
They never finish, they never even begin.

No grammatical *sentence*
To contain experience, to pierce chaos.
Crying in pidgin Pigeon into the wind:

Coo coo Hoo-hoo Hro-coo— a crazy credo—

—so mumbled a curmudgeon,
his feathers ruffled,
sitting on a city bench

EROTIC LANDSCAPE

Sand dunes and rounded rocks, naked, untouched, unseen
(How do you call them in your country,
masculine or feminine?) *Feminine*:
for a thousand years she
she never knew any lying promises
nor the good intentions, which can lie worse.

The voice of nature, its melody, it cacophony
(how do you designate it in your nation,
he or she?) *He*:
he raved and rained, drenched and lapped
her every crevice, limb, and creek.

The rocks reverberated, echoing wind-vowel moans.
The dunes reconfigured, hollowing mounds itno mouths.
The land became a living tongue,
A singing sensuality, never by man or woman sung.

Raining At Gettysburg

Buried are the dead and living are the tears.
Who cried those tears?—
Honest Abe long ago or a drunken tourist B—?
A. or B.? It's nobody's tears. The rain
Is simply raining, raining just like that,
Lightly raining on the battlefields.

Also on every field raining, over the monuments
And raining in the parlour
Wherever whoever is drenched through and through,
Soaked under heavenly allotments of pain,
Of mortality, and seeming no mercy.
So died our martyrs, so died Abe,
Fighting against having fought in vain.
Died unable to prevent it.

Benny peruses the *Gettysburg Historical Pamphlet,*
As a bloodred stain dribbles down his unshaven beard.
(Closer inspection would reveal it to be vin ordinaire.)

*

Laying down the pamphlet, not right for reading on holiday,
Benny knows he should care—nose-shooed—but what
With all the other matter and stuff, not to mention....
Resolved, soldierly, noble his brow,
He resurrects the pamphlet!
...and again he snoozes, and it slips down.

*

Benny makes a mat of the pamphlet
On a bench wet with the enamels of rain.
He mutters:
> *If a guy's gotta drink this rotgut,*
> *he must be some kinda martyr.*
He wonders if he should meet Abe himself,
What say, how address him?
> *Th'others stank, like this cheapo wine,*
> *But you made a better, uh, oh, whatever,*
> *come rain or come shine.*

> *If only that damn rain would stop.*
Saying it, the red drizzles down his shirt.

*

Should the Presbyterian lady under the umbrella
Who sits on the bench across and disapproves
Hold for her book *The Red Badge of Courage,*
Her presence would be, symbolically,
Convenient. Regrettably,
She's not the spectator for our purposes:
Not with her fingery bones on the Bible
Tapping relentlessly.

MEN'S HEAD, CITY BUS STATION

Braingone old bums
argue with the air

Runaways not changing clothes
in the mirror change their moods

A drunk and another drunk:
"Piss on you." "Piss on you!"

A fat pervert, jelly in tight pants,
masturbates in open stall number three

Fluorescent light, it coats the eye,
like urine on dirty white tiles

The cops joke with each other
even as those fucks with badges arrest you

HELOISE

THE WHORISH HELOISE

Sisters May, Mary and Joy
    chatter or laugh
Till the noon is buzzing
    in the animal sound of it.
On and on they chirp like birds:
    about birds they sigh,
Buttered noodles on the Sabbath,
    or blistered feet of the Son of Love
Not even the Baptizer was fit to sandal.
    How innocent are these:
They are as innocent as daisies
    they gather in morning's moist fields:
But their chatter preys
    on the milk in my breast
Which turns now sour, sweet Abelard.
    Prayers and sin, the only ornaments
This forsaken whore will wear.

HELOISE'S FOUNTAIN PEN

Stars seem deceptious moths that graze
As nuns kneel to pray.
But you dare not utter what they pray or say.
Tears and talks and the stars may be washed
In the tears and talk of nuns. Far below
Cows nibble in nun's cowls the grass
Where Abelard walked.
        Now over field and flesh the deluge comes.
Returned is your room to the dusk tide of flesh:
You sit through its flood, and evening's anchor grasp—
This feather that was once Simon the goose.
Down as feathers fall white images of Abelard.
His thought is so high none can know it.
Who can climb so tall a mountain?
Fetch Simon the goose to fly over it.
Quill call him, let the shadow of a feather....

Heloise, Adieu

I loved thee and whom I so did
    I called my man and I his whore.
I was the peasant maid
      who brought milk to the king.
But a king dies on Tuesday
       and the living man eats slop.
Discourse again on the soul, Abelard,
        tell me why yours there is here.
I loved a man but least
     did I love the man in him;
Rather love the fit of the distracted moon,
       love moonlight when no shadows move.
Your breath fed on mine, fragrant,
      as the flowers the calves chewed
While dusk the church bells tolled
       Till the hour the cow lows and reclines.
Through the cold night I sleep alone.

Dada Lullaby

Sleep inside a fat, fat whale
Sleep deep, deep as a fairy tale
Why, whale slept in a fairy tale
    Silly little whale
    Silly fairy tale
    Sweet milk's in the pail
White pail   white whale   white fairy tale

I'm sleeping

    — imitated from the Flemish
      of Paul van Ostaijen

THE GARDEN

Free soul in a prisoned hour
Happy spirit in an unhappy place
A tree in bud along a ghetto street

Was she merely mortal, human like us?
Gnostic beauty: bending to earth, without freight
Nearby, unespied, young St. Christian hurried on

Old earth memories may flood the mind
Of a young girl, clothed in her nakedness,
Sleeping to an open window, where an old tree blooms

And where flowers never grew grow there flowers
An old owl amid the branches wakes
And flies darkward grazing her uneasy dreams

> *She in that garden planted be agayne*
> *And grows afresh, as she had never seene*
> *Fleshy corruption, nor mortal payne*

A window-box garden hangs over the street
On the street below, garbage and grime
Over it: geraniums, girls, and grief

I do not know her name.

A Tiny Advertisement

Now how would it be
If a dwarf, bumping against a giant!
Up-jumps on the giant's toenail,
Hurries out his tools, carving and scraping away,
And in that dense plastic toenail
Builds for himself a trim bungalow.
Now how would it be?

It would be very nice if
If a little girl I know
Who eats chocolates, who loves chocolates,
Would save the aluminum wrap
And make silver curtains, silver tablecloths.

OLD-FASHIONED MARRIAGE-TRICK BALLAD

Even as evening
      darkened dense as an olive
(Plucked from a tree planted
      below two stars in the forest),
Then was there Jane-a-dreams
      by my fire sadly humming,
Till the notes kissed in my ear
      as might a delirious woman.
Was I deceived, or did I watch
      a witchy swaying back and forth
As slow sad music danced in the flames.
Mother of God but a man's alone.
      Here finds the forbidden gipsy floor
      Through startled spectacles a vision stirs:
      It's round and around
      And around and around
      The far foot flies up and the left leg lies down.

The measure of steps they were tracing
      left strokes like calligraphy
That was written for animals
      and read at risk of lunacy.
Nonsense words that Jane hummed
      harped my fortunes it seemed,
Random notes that she piped
      melodized the woman I craved.
For yes it's I know
      that my heart fell out
The time that I watched
      while this nutty lady waltzed.
      It's round and around
      And around and around
      Her far foot flies up while soft she dips down.

This report I then labored
        and subsequently polish
Not for for your ridicule
        and least for your knowledge.
I wrote it only to prove
        that I knew to write,
That on her looked a learning
        she should profit to scan.
Such was my plot
        this murky lady to woo,
My fate became this lady
        for my own to have won.
                You'll find somewhere this forbidden floor
                On its grass you'll watch your new bride whirl
                And it round and round a new vision stirs

Now far from our campfire
        worn stars have grown chilly,
Far away from that firelight
        our love has turned weary.
I have my wife
        but a heart full of woes,
I have children
        but toils and nothing to show.
Yet sometimes though sad,
        sad and slow in the dusk,
I hear piped the tune
        that Jane-a-dreams piped once:
                And it's round and around
                And around and around
                The weary soul flies up
                When a worn body lies down.

Waiting For Phil In The Austin Bus Station

Hadn't seen Cousin Phil in hell
Of a long time—sin of omission.
So hopped the proletarian bus
To Austin, to end the reign/rain of missing years.

Late he was to come fetch me.
To wile away the minutes, patient with impatience,
I practiced fantasy: Anyone who entered the station
Could, would be Phil, subtly, or grossly, altered
By time's mischief: magical transmogrification
    —playful imaginings!—

First person through the door barely squeezed through:
275 or 300 lbs of waddling pulchritude.
    —"Sexy Sadie, Fat Lady"—
"Why, Phil, packed on a few pounds lately?
Or *pregnant*? you breakthrough naughty boy."

Next to cross the doorway, a strikingly handsome black man.
    —"Black Is Beautiful"—
"Wow, Phil, that is the mother of all suntans!
Your mirror must be in love with you."

Next, minutes later, entered an erotic stereotype—
Hubba-hubba: hair dyed blonde, scarlet lipstick,
    — purple eye-shadow, tight tangerine frock—
"At last expressing your secret
Crossover dreams, Phyllis? I knew it all along."

And then who should come in but himself.
He had in appearance hardly changed at all.
It felt good to see Phil again.

HOW TO WRITE A POEM CALLED "CAVALIER"

Mention Venus: lashes flutter & blushes flush.
All undergarments are silken and their descent floorwards
Shall fill your stanzas with a windy sibilance
"Hush" — Eden's hither-thithering snakelike S.

Pale and wan, fond lover? delighting in dress disarray?
Once in a long-ago of danger and gallantry and play
Cavalier poets composed odes to Beauty's soul—
A metaphor for coy women and Desire overriding rules.

Erase the centuries, now it's your turn to grind out some idea.
Perchance copy a cavalier and call Death "a dream—of her."
Sadly your poem needs to wake. But how?—
In this crumbling epilogue of too little and too much.

Lust and deceit are but grown-up toys. The rhyme—?
Joy! Obviously, joy. Was it once more joyful?
Recall yourself young, reading 17th C and copying Cavalier wit,
Did you think then: the Laws excused, recused you The Poet?

JAHRZEIT

My father, Leon Paine, is two years dead
As the green leaves come again in springtime.
No one was sweeter, dearer (now two years dead)
As we grasp at the here-and-now flowering sweetly.

You hardly perceived your own virtues,
Nor boasted that you, in fact, had any:
Instead, were humorous; and precise in detail, your most elegance.
Strain was beyond you, you never exaggerated

But accepted, & saw, in the plain, the good
Of everyone clearly—indeed saw dearly,
So you could utter the poignant truth
So mildly, it shed its poison.

Fuss and glory make a noisy commotion,
You simply liked what what-is usually brought you.
This "poem," without merit, would have pleased you,
As did your daughter, wife, son, and most others.

If any is at peace, you are that any
(— I do not know where religion would have you —).
If the difficult can be accepted, it's in part thanks to you,
Though you demurred. "I was helpless to do other. "
                                        Now in spring greening.

BE A BEE

Gorge yourself on reds and purples,
Live the life that's fresh and weightless.

Every day is drunk with honey,
Every way is sleepy circles,
Every sage is buzzing, humming.

REMEMBER THE NIGHT YOU SLEPT IN GOD

A BAD NIGHT'S SLEEP

Remember how you refused to look at the clock,
dreaded the night, found the tangled sheets obscene,
Insomnia outmaneuvers, outweighs every hope,
Damn them, the drawers bare of ZzzQuil or valium
at 3 a. m., or 4, when exhausted is every thought,
lack of sleep, some uncommitted crime confessing

A GOOD NIGHTS SLEEP

Winter outside was freezing,
the apt. was cool, but under the blankets was warming.
Your arthritic body would never feel twenty,
having just made love or won a blue ribbon,
yet the bed lay inviting, a white beach dozing,
pale waters lapping/ the radio softly humming.

DOZING AFTER NOON

It was simple as drinking apple juice
Or sneaking ice cream. The sun felt nice and harmless,
And all around you all its rays were emanating,
Warming each of your cells, and the dust in the air
Was soporific, sleep-educing. And nowhere to sleep
But here, and so you napped soundly.

BIOGRAPHICAL NOTE

This book of poems may be unique, in one way. Jeffery Paine spent nearly sixty years (!) working on this, his first collection—for six decades in odd hours writing and rewriting, reworking and revising, honing and beginning anew. JP decided not to publish a single poem till this small-scale whole shebang was ready; also he tried not to write what might be, in essence, the same poem twice. (JP, with the Nobel Prize-winning poet Joseph Brodsky, did however edit a fat anthology of modern international poems: *The Poetry of Our World*.)

In other genres JP published widely but he may be best known for ushering Eastern culture and spirituality to popular audiences in the West. "Jeffery Paine is an unusual voice in American letters," so observed Indian novelist and Undersecretary General of the United Nations Shashi Tharoor, "one steeped in the wisdom of the East and yet infused with a knowing and witty sensibility that is profoundly Western."

Although JP's books *Father India, Re-enchantment: Tibetan Buddhism Comes to the West*, and *Enlightenment Town* were each named in various media a "Best Book of the Year," they didn't make him rich, i. e. provide a livable income. He thus indulged his penchant for working in older buildings.

JP helped manage the oldest hotel in Amsterdam (dating from 1654). He worked in advertising, partly because the office was the oldest house in San Francisco (converted). He edited a magazine in the Smithsonian Castle in Washington DC, his office being where once Abraham Lincoln came to view official parades. He taught specialized literature in Descartes' bedroom. That's about the respectable side of it.

Since *Eternity, Speak with This Living Man* took six decades, JP's next book of poetry, if published, will be published in a parallel universe.

www.ingramcontent.com/pod-product-compliance
Lightning Source LLC
Chambersburg PA
CBHW011218120626
46545CB00008B/3054